# Finding Faith

## A young woman's journey from darkness to light

Lynn Archer

# DEDICATION

To my Baba Jee, who first showed me the love of a
father and, though he caused me pain, protected
me from so much.

# AUTHOR'S NOTE

Jesus truly is a miracle worker. In June of 2017, I (Lynn) was given the opportunity to meet Rebekah for the first time at a mutual friend's house. I have always had a heart for the persecuted Church and a desire and willingness to write, and Rebekah had been hoping and praying that God would bring her someone to turn her life into a book. It didn't take long for "Finding Faith" to begin.

And so, we began. While finishing my Bachelor's degree and interning at my church, I would meet with Rebekah twice a month to hear her story and start putting it down on paper. Caribou Coffee turned out to be the perfect place to meet, and we had many a smoothie and coffee there.

This book has taught me so much about the love and faithfulness of God, and I pray that Jesus reveals to you exactly what you need through this book.

Lynn Archer

# PREFACE
By Rebekah

"See, I have written your name on the palms of my hands." (Isaiah 49:16)

A year from June 2017 marked the beginning of a precious friendship with Lynn...started through Jesus.. He used my friend Mary who I met only 2 months beforehand!!

Both Mary & Lynn have been used by the Holy Spirit to make this book happen...

This is a product of what happens when God does Supernatural!

He equipped us for His Kingdom because He loves us so much!

*The names within this story have been changed to protect the privacy of the individuals involved.*

# CONTENTS

# CHAPTER ONE:
# THE BEGINNING

*And the peace of God, which surpasses all*
*understanding, will guard your hearts and your minds*
*in Christ Jesus.*
*Philippians 4:7*

## Early Years

My name is Rebekah, but I am merely the teller of the story, not the reason it's being told. This story is about Jesus, and it always has been, though I didn't know it was Him at the beginning.

And where is the beginning? Well, the beginning was many years ago, when God first began creating out of the depths of his love. The story continued, even through the brokenness of humanity, up to the crucifixion of Jesus himself. But even then, the salvation of all those who would love Jesus and choose him was not the end of the story. It merely leads up to when I joined it.

My part began when I was born, the eldest child in a well-off Muslim family in Southwest Asia. You can see Jesus working even from my birth— I was born in the only Christian hospital in the nation, and it was a nun that handed me to my mother after I was born! Our God is such a God of detail, is he not?

Within the next twelve years, two younger brothers joined our family: Sarmad and Raheem. Raheem, the middle child, was quiet and laid back, while Sarmad, the youngest, was loud and boisterous. Together, the five of us formed a family. Both our parents were both very involved in our lives (though I have always been a daddy's girl), helping us with homework, friends, and navigating different cultures at the International School. Regardless of how often the many cultures came into conflict, our lives were influenced by the West as much as by Asia. I grew up on lasagna and brownies, not only curry, and spoke English as well as I spoke my native tongue.

My family was Muslim, as I mentioned, but it wasn't an enforced lifestyle that they thrust upon me. Hijabs and daily prayers were certainly encouraged, but they weren't required, and so I didn't choose to take part. That being said, at age three I was memorizing the Quran in ancient Arabic; though we weren't consistent in practicing Islam, we were still Muslims.

By age two, I was attending preschool at the International School, and by the time I reached high school, I was a very successful student. At the prompting of my counselor, I took the TOEFL and SAT, and when I scored highly on both, my counselor helped me choose and apply to seven different American universities. When I was accepted into all seven, I remember sitting back thrilled that I had been accepted and even offered scholarships, but overwhelmed because I had no idea how to choose what college I should attend. So I went to my father, as I always did.

After looking at all seven universities, their costs, and their offers, my dad chose a college in St. Paul, MN. It was an all-girls school, which my dad found important, as he didn't trust American men, or even Americans in general. His next words have stayed with me even to today; "Stay away from those American people!" he said, "They will corrupt you! They are bad people, they are sinners! Everybody is a sinner. Everybody is bad. The girls talk on the phone with their boyfriends for hours. They drink and smoke, they go to nightclubs! Stay away from all of them!"

As I boarded the plane to America with my mother, I was excited to start this new chapter of independence and adventure, but I was terrified of the bad Americans. Adding to that fear was the fact that although I longed for independence, I couldn't do simple tasks by myself. Having been raised in a wealthy family, servants did everything for us. I wasn't accustomed to making my bed or doing laundry. I let my mother know that I was fairly certain I wasn't going to make it on my own, but nonetheless, the time came for her to go home, and thus began my college career on the other side of the world.

I took my father's words seriously. My roommate was exactly what he had warned me about— talking on the phone for hours to her boyfriend, drinking, smoking, going to nightclubs— and it only confirmed my fears. Anxiety had been my companion all throughout my childhood, and I fell into a routine of going to class, to the cafeteria (which did not have very good food, by the way), to the library, and to my bed. And that was it. Class, cafeteria, library, bed. Class, cafeteria, library, bed. Over and over again. Soon a year passed, and I had done as my father had said and stayed away. I had no friends on this continent, and the loneliness was starting to sink in. But I remembered my father's warning, and I continued to stay away. Year two came and went. Class, cafeteria, library, bed. Class, cafeteria, library, bed. As year three started, the pain of loneliness only grew, but my fear of being corrupted still overrode my desire for connection, and so I continued to keep to myself.

## Jesus is God

By this time, my roommate situation had changed in that now, all my roommates were internationals like me, but they still did what my father had warned against; drinking, partying and spending too much time with their boyfriends. But these roommates were not content to let me isolate myself. One night, as they were getting ready to go to a house party, one of them invited me to come.

"Nooooo, no thank you. I don't like what you do there, and I don't want anything to do with it," I said, hearing my father in my refusal.

"You can come with us and not do any of that! You don't have to do the stuff you don't like— we just don't want to leave you alone," she replied. Her offer seemed innocent enough, and oh how I desired to be *with* people again. . .

It didn't take much more pushing before I was convinced. My desire for relationship had finally taken over my fear of corruption. But when we arrived at the party, I immediately regretted my decision. Music, spewing more profanities than melodies, blared out through speakers which made it too loud to talk to anyone, but that didn't even matter considering everyone was drunk out of their minds. Everywhere I looked, alcohol was pouring down throats, cigarettes and other drugs were making no attempt to hide, and many acts that belong behind closed doors after marriage vows were happening right in the middle of the living room. I looked around the house party, feeling terribly out of place as the only sober person in the building. Sitting in the middle of this environment, I felt even more alone than I had in the library. Eventually, after sitting alone for a while, the hostess approached me.

"Can I getcha anything to drink there, friend?" she asked, her words slurring slightly from too much alcohol.

"Water, please," I answered, determined not to be corrupted, even though I had agreed to come to a house party.

"Sorry, friend, but I don't have any water with me right now. . ." She paused and looked at the drinks she had in her hand. "Here ya go, have this one," she finally said, holding out a bottle to me. "It doesn't have very much alcohol, so you don't have to worry about getting drunk or nuthin."

I took the bottle hesitantly and studied it for a moment, wondering if it was worth it. I was thirsty though, and she said I wouldn't get drunk. . . so I took a sip. And it was good. So I took another sip. Soon I had finished off the bottle and gotten another one. Before we left the house party, I had finished five bottles of what I found out later were wine coolers, and I was extremely drunk. My roommates and I left the party to go to a nightclub, where any reservations I had maintained previously all fell away. I sang and danced and acted like a fool, just like everyone else there. Soon I caught the eye of a man named John, a man whose family had just come to America from South America. His mother had been Hindu and his father a Muslim, but they had all found Jesus. John, however, was wandering, not walking with Jesus.

He moved in with me, and soon, we were the ones doing the things my father had warned me about. In a matter of months, I went from being a good Muslim girl, refusing to leave my standards, to becoming pregnant out of wedlock.

As I veered further off-course though, John started to veer back. He began pursuing Christ again, and we went to a bookstore and got a KJV Bible; the first I had ever laid eyes on. However, for all the truth contained between those covers, not a word of it made sense to me. I didn't understand it, nor did I know what to do with it. John soon began realizing just how lost I was and so he invited me to a week-long Christian conference with his family. It was at this conference that I heard for the first time that Jesus is God.

And it made sense.

At the end of the week, I prayed the sinner's prayer along with many others, but I didn't mean it. I was overwhelmed by the truth, but I wasn't ready to commit, to choose Christ over me. Along with the incredible truth I had been exposed to, which I was still wrapping my head around and wrestling with, I lost my baby that week. I was reeling. I was lost. What was truth? What was life? Who is this Jesus? What was right?

I was a mess. A complete and total mess. I wasn't a disaster waiting to happen— I was already a disaster and trying to pick up the pieces while the tornado still whirled around me. I no longer had any solid footing— my family was on the other side of the world, and there was no way I could tell them about what I had been doing; my friends were not equipped with the answers and support that I needed, and I had no other community to turn to. As if this wasn't enough, John and I drifted apart during that season, It was at this point that I took out a Bible and a Quran and laid them next to each other in front of me.

"What is true? Where is God?" I asked, staring at the books in front of me. "Who are you?"

I wanted so desperately for a sign. I wanted to believe in Him, to believe that Jesus was more than a prophet, that he was God. I longed for the Bible to be truth, and yet, I wasn't sure. Years of Islam had already laid their foundation.

It was not a conclusion I could come to by myself. It was one that I needed to come to by God revealing himself and He did. Jesus, my sweet Jesus, began revealing himself to me, showing me who he really was.

## Conversion

Not long after I had sat down with the Bible and Quran, one of my friends, a Christian, invited me to come to church with her. I was unsure, because even though I knew that church would be a good place to learn more about Jesus, I was a dorm advisor, and I was on duty that Sunday morning. I went back and forth all week, but Jesus knew I needed some encouragement to go.

"Wake up, Rebekah, you have to go to church!" a loud, clear voice proclaimed on the morning of February 22nd, 1998, jerking me from my sleep that Sunday morning. I jumped, startled by the sudden voice in my empty room.

"Who was that?" I muttered to myself as I scoured my room, searching under my bed, out the window, in the closet. Nothing. I wanted to assume that it was some random stranger who happened to know my name, or a friend who was really good at hiding, but I couldn't ignore it. But then I heard it again. And again. The voice came back, telling me the same thing.

"Rebekah, you have to go to church!"

"Rebekah, you have to go to church!"

"Rebekah, you have to go to church!"

Eventually, after having turned my apartment inside out trying to find the voice, I decided that I should just go to church. I called my friend, and she picked me up and took me.

Once at church, with the preacher well underway in his message, the only thing I was hearing is "You're a sinner. You're a sinner. You're a sinner." I didn't like it, nor did I fully understand it, so instead I went to the children's ministry. As I walked in, a simple but joyful song was playing, and all the kids were singing and dancing with it.

"Mercy is falling, is falling, is falling. Mercy it falls like the sweet, spring rain. Mercy is falling, is falling all over me."

While I enjoyed watching them dance, I was confident that I would never dance like them and make a fool of myself. Soon, I was not watching the kids bouncing with their hands up; *I* was the one bouncing and dancing and singing!

"What's wrong with me?" I kept thinking as I would jump again and again, wondering what had come over me to make me dance like this. "I just said I would never do this!"

I continued to jump and dance through the rest of the songs, unstoppable. After the service was over, my friend and I were approached by an elderly woman named Evelyn, who invited us over to her place for lunch. My friend and I immediately looked at each other and said in unison: "FREE FOOD!!!"

The offer of food was all it took for us to agree to come out to her place. She sat us down at the table, but none of the food had been set out yet, even though our hostess was already seated. We sat in silence for a long five minutes. I was wondering what exactly was going on, as we had been offered food, and now that we were here, there was no food. Water hadn't even made it to the table yet.

"Rebekah, will you say grace?" Evelyn finally asked.

Silence resumed. The clock continued ticking, we continued breathing, and thoughts continued to dance through my head. Why was she asking me to say grace? I was not a Christian— surely she knew that! But then she had only just met me. . . but then she should be able to figure out by my silence. . .

Another five minutes had passed before I finally spoke. "Evelyn," I finally said, "I cannot say grace because I am not a Christian."

"I don't believe that!" Evelyn exclaimed immediately, "I see Jesus Christ all around you. He is knocking on the door of your heart!"

As she finished speaking, I could hear the speaker from the conference all those months ago. "Behold! I stand at the door and knock! If anyone hears my voice and opens the door, I will come in and eat with them, and they with me."

Even while those words were still racing through my memory, my heart began to react to the knocking. I could literally feel my heart being knocked on as it pounded in my chest, loud and hard. Colors danced before my eyes. I was suddenly overwhelmed with the understanding that the love of Abba was *real*, and the love of Abba was *good*. Joy rushed into me like a waterfall and poured out my eyes. I was shaking— no, jumping— on the chair, overcome by the goodness and love of Jesus.

Evelyn ran for her Bible, and we read through the entire book of John that day. I let each word soak into me like I was bathing in the truth. Jesus is the Light. He is the Truth. He is the Son. He is Love.

I still don't know whether or not I ate that day, but for the first time, I was fed.

## CHAPTER TWO:
## JOURNEY TO MY HOME

*"The eye is the lamp of the body. So, if your eye is*
*healthy, your whole body will be full of light,*
*Matthew 6:22*

**My Baptism**

I continued to meet with Evelyn from that
point on, and she helped me lay the foundation for
my faith. Through her life, she showed me what
being a follower of Jesus meant and passed on her
wisdom to me. She walked me through the
differences between simply being a believer in
Jesus versus pursuing him wholeheartedly, and
told me that it was the pursuit, the willingness to
be like Abraham and leave everything behind for
Jesus, that made someone a Christian. It wasn't a
matter of salvation, but a matter of trust. How far
were you willing to go for Christ? Would you
merely be a believer in Jesus, or would you be a
Christian?

As I grew in my faith, I was determined to
give God my all, and was given no shortage of

opportunities to pursue Jesus wholeheartedly in my reactions to life. As Evelyn pushed me, the Holy Spirit drew me to react in worship. Anger? No, worship. Fear? No, worship. Sadness? Worship. The Holy Spirit taught me how to draw the line between acknowledging my God-given emotions and letting them rule me. While many a curveball was thrown my way that year, easily the hardest thing I walked through was getting diagnosed with spinocerebellar ataxia, a rare and (medically) incurable genetic disorder. The news was devastating to me and my family, but I quickly found comfort in the arms of the Father. The promises that He had made suddenly came to life, and I began to simply believe what He said. He is not a liar, after all. Verses like "O Lord my God, I cried to you for help, and you have healed me" (Psalm 30:2) became real to me. He makes such simple promises, and they are everywhere in His Word, but they all boil down to this: Ask, and you will receive. Seek, and you will find. Knock, and the door will be open to you. He delights to provide, and even if he didn't provide immediate healing, I knew (and know) that he will provide whatever is best for me, even if the best for me isn't healing.

Knowing hope itself, I could not help but pour out into others. Despite my hard circumstances, I had the Holy Spirit with me, so what had I to fear? I became an active member of my church, joining my church's bussing ministry where we would go pick up kids from the inner city and bring them to church activities. We would pick up kids in pajamas, kids who had been waiting all week to come back, all kinds of kids from all kinds of situations. I also joined the Evangelism Explosion— a ministry that met on Saturdays and just walked the streets, being led by the Holy Spirit to evangelize and minister to anyone and everyone and going door to door to share the love of Christ.

Over the next two and a half years, I kept my faith a secret from my family. Though I clung to God's promises, fear had already planted its seeds deep in my heart and it continued to grow. As a Muslim family, they not only had the right to kill me, they were expected to. According to the Quran and our country's laws and culture, I either needed to convert back to Islam or die, and I had no intentions of abandoning Jesus.

However scary the thought of my family finding out was, God was still bigger and continued to move in radical ways. It was during this time that I would be baptized.

The Easter baptism service was only a couple weeks away, but to be baptized, you first needed to take a month long course to make sure that you understood why you were being baptized and what it meant to do so. However, Jesus had told me that I was going to be baptized on Easter Sunday, so I started talking to John's dad about it. By this point we had established a good relationship with each other, outside of my former relationship with John. I had gained favor in his eyes with my passion for Jesus and my willingness to serve in whatever capacity I was asked, but that did not change his stance when I asked if I could be baptized on Easter.

"Rebekah," he said, "you know that you have to take a one-month class before you can be baptized, and it's only five days before Easter!"

"I need to be baptized— I don't care what it takes!" I told him, determined to be baptized. The conversation went back and forth— I need to be baptized, you need to take the class.

"How about you meet with the elder, Mr. Finley, tomorrow, and see if he can make it happen?" he finally conceded. I was ecstatic. I happily agreed and the meeting was arranged.

The next day, Wednesday, I walked into Mr. Finley's office, and we proceeded to repeat the conversation that I had had with John's dad the day before.

"Alright, Rebekah, I can see that you are determined to be baptized. How about you memorize Romans 6:1-5 and come back in two days and say it to me, and give me a visual of what it means."

I happily agreed, and no memorization had ever come so easily to me. I returned in two days time and once again, sat down in his office.

"So, Rebekah, can you say those verses for me?" he asked.

"What shall we say, then? Shall we go on sinning so that grace may increase? By no means! We are those who have died to sin; how can we live in it any longer? Or don't you know that all of us who were baptized into Christ Jesus were baptized into his death? We were therefore buried with him through baptism into death in order that, just as Christ was raised from the dead through the glory of the Father, we too may live a new life. For if we have been united with him in a death like his, we will certainly also be united with him in a resurrection like his," I said, not missing a beat.

Mr. Finley paused for a moment, caught off-guard by my quick memorization and recital of Scripture. "How did you memorize that so quickly?" he finally asked.

"When the Holy Spirit wants something to happen, nothing will stand in his way!" I responded, smiling.

"Amen to that! What about the visual? Can you give me a picture of what this means?" he asked.

"I see green, green everywhere, and I am in the Garden of Eden, chasing butterflies with children all around me. It is all beautiful and perfect— and then I am suddenly unable to walk. I sit down on a wheelchair and a man comes— Jesus— and holds the wheelchair steady. He then turns the wheelchair and we go shooting off into the sky, into a crown of thorns. He continues to go, pushing the wheelchair up into heaven. We sit up in heaven together for a moment and then He takes me back down to earth, down to the Garden again, where I am able to stand once more and I start dancing with Jesus and the children."

"Rebekah, you are going to be baptized on Sunday and not only that, but you need to give a ten minute testimony so we can videotape it!" Mr. Finley exclaimed.

I was elated. I practically jumped out of my seat trying to thank him and I felt like dancing on my way back home, but even that was nothing compared to how I felt after actually being baptized. I felt new— like a baby— and I wanted to feel that way for the rest of my life. I had been made a new creation in Christ, I was a beloved daughter and cherished child of the King. What greater gifts could there be?

## Secrets Revealed

After my baptism, my faith continued to flourish. I loved Jesus, I loved those around me, and I loved my home country. I began to ask God to send me back so that I could show the love of Jesus to those living under the fear of Islam. Isaiah 6:8 began to resound in me, like it was the very beat of my heart. "And I heard the voice of the Lord saying, 'Whom shall I send, and who will go for us?' Then I said, 'Here I am! Send me.'" Send me Lord, send me. I became desperate to go back to my home country to share with my people who Jesus was and how much he loves them.

God certainly heard my prayers and was setting things in motion across the ocean, but in the meantime, I was majoring in Speech Education. When God kept speaking to me about Proverbs 22:6 "Train up a child in the way he should go; even when he is old he will not depart from it," I added on a minor in Early Childhood Education. By now I was on my last semester at college. Though the end of college was nearing, my faith was firmly grounded and I was looking forward to see what God had for me in the future.

Two months before my graduation, one of my mom's friends started asking around if there was anyone who would work at her preschool at the International School. It didn't take long for her to connect the dots (or really, for Jesus to connect the dots) and approach my mom to ask about me. Knowing that I was getting my minor in Early Childhood Education, and having seen me work with children, she got my email from my mom and without telling me, started interviewing me over email. From my side of things, it just looked like she was making conversation, and I didn't even realize what her goal was until numerous emails had been exchanged and then one came in congratulating me on being hired! I prayed about it and accepted the position gladly, excited to have a good job right out of college, but even more than that, I was excited to go back to my home. My dad was going to bring the contract to me to be signed when he came for my graduation, and then bring it back as I was not leaving right away.

When it came time for my graduation, my dad and Sarmad came to my beloved Minnesota to celebrate. John's parents, Tim and Carrie, were kind enough to open up their home to my family, so my father and brother stayed with them for the time they were in Minnesota. As I still had not breathed a word of my faith to my family, I had spent many hours talking to Tim and Carrie about timing and about how I needed to tell them, but I also needed to tell them at the right place and time. I asked them not to tell my family that I was a Christian, but to let Holy Spirit point out the time to me so that I would be the one to tell them. Both Tim and Carrie had agreed, and though I was nervous about how family would react, I trusted that my Jesus would take care of me. I had spent the week before their arrival fasting, seeking God about his timing and asking that it be revealed.

One afternoon, as Carrie was making tuna sandwiches for lunch, my father started talking to her while I was outside.

"So, you and my daughter are very close, yes?"

"Yes, yes we are," Carrie responded with a smile.

"How often do you see Rebekah?" he asked.

"Oh, nearly every Sunday," she answered, mixing the tuna. It was all my father needed.

Without another word he turned and walked back up to his room. Moments later, I walked in.

"Rebekah," she said, "*this* was the right time!"

When she had relayed the conversation back to me, I ran after him, praying every step of the way. *Jesus, help me. Help my family.*

I hesitated just outside their door and caught the last bits of their conversation.

"Do you know she's a Christian?" the deep voice of my father asked.

"Yes," I heard my brother say. "Carrie told me everything."

I took a deep breath, a wave of fear and pain passing over me as I realized that Carrie had done the one thing I had asked her not to do. *Sweet Jesus, please help me. I need you now.*

I knocked softly on the door and gently pushed it open. When neither my father nor my brother responded, I sat down quietly on the floor. My brother didn't move his head from his hands; my father refused to look at anything other than the ceiling. No one spoke. No one had words. In their eyes, I had betrayed them in the worst way possible. I had left my father's teaching, my mother's raising. I had brought shame on my family and committed a crime worse than what my father had warned me about all those years ago. And yet, what I had done was the absolute best thing I could ever have done with my life.

Agonizing moments passed as all these thoughts glided through my brain. *Jesus, what do you want me to do? I don't know.* Suddenly Evelyn's words came back to me. Enter in as a servant, enter in with humility, for a gentle word turns away anger.

"Can I get you water?" I finally asked, my quiet words breaking the fragile silence.

"Rebekah," my father said, his voice shaking, "I have one question for you. Are you a Muslim or a Christian?"

"Neither," I answered, thinking back to Evelyn again.

"What do you mean?"

"I am a believer in the Lord Jesus Christ."

With that, my father bolted out of the room, ran out of the house, and took off down the road. I chased him down to the porch, screaming for him to come back, crying for my daddy to return. Tim stopped by my side momentarily to tell me that it might be better if he talked to my dad instead of me, and then chased after the quickly disappearing figure of my father.

Carrie made some phone calls, and almost half of my church came over, praying and interceding with us in her living room. I was so thankful for being part of such a wonderful family as the family of Christ, but couldn't help but mourn the breaking of the family I had been born into.

We worshiped, we prayed, we cried out. For hours we brought my family before God until finally my father came back with Tim. He didn't say a word to me— just kept walking right on up the stairs back to his room. We continued to pray and seek God, to present the situation before him and ask him to move.

He and my brother stayed in Minnesota for another two weeks before it was time to leave. Although I had been fearful and anxious before they knew that I loved Jesus, once they knew, I was completely at peace. It was all in Jesus hands, and now there was nothing left to hide, no trying to plan out the timing. It was completely out of my hands. My only option would be to renounce Jesus, but that simply wasn't an option for me. No amount of pain or fear was worth giving up my Jesus.

During my father's stay in Minnesota, he remained cordial to me and went with me wherever I asked him to go, but adamantly refused to go to church with me. There was now a distinction between my father and I, and though we both loved each other dearly, neither of us were willing to change our beliefs for the other.

Graduation came and went, as did my family. My father and brother soon left for New York to drop off my brother for him to start college. I had a few precious weeks with my Minnesota family before it was time for me to come home, back to Asia. My mother and youngest brother, Sarmad, came to pick me up.

After showing them some of my favorite spots, I asked them to go to church, just as I had with my dad. Lo and behold— my mother said yes! She came to church with me that Sunday and listened to Christians talk about Jesus and watch them love Him. It was incredible, and yet that was not the end of their trip.

They met all my friends, and joined in all the goodbyes. At one point, my church was having a farewell party for me, and my mother and brother attended. At this farewell party, the focus was totally on Jesus, not on saying goodbye to me, and it couldn't possibly have been any more perfect. Worship— such sweet worship, spontaneous and pure— filled the room with heavenly melodies and shameless tears. People stood to give testimonies of the goodness of God in their lives. Others knelt on the floor and poured out their hearts to Jesus. It was beautiful. It was real. It was perfect. And my Muslim brother and mother were there to witness it all.

Just a few short nights later, we were at the airport. Some of my closest friends had come with me to put off saying goodbye until the very last second. As my best friend, Whitney, told me through tears that she didn't want me to leave because she knew I would be hurt, I realized that this was the moment that I was choosing to give everything up for Jesus. I could back out and stay in America. I didn't have to leave Minnesota. I could stay and be surrounded by my brothers and sisters in Christ and get a job here and avoid the persecution I knew would come for me. But even as I looked into her fearful eyes, red from crying, I only became more certain that no matter the cost, I would follow my Jesus anywhere.

# CHAPTER THREE:
# MEETING MISSIONARIES

*Where two or three are gathered in my name, there I am among them.*
*Matthew 18:20*

## New Life in an Old Place

"This is *not* America!" my father told me the first day I was back. "You will *not* talk to other Christians, you will *not* go to church, you will *not* read a Bible— nothing!"

My father, however adamant he was about the rules, will be the first to tell you that when I have set my mind to something, nothing will stop me. But however determined I was to continue to walk out my faith, being a Christian in a Muslim country is a whole different ball game than being a Christian in America. It wasn't just that my father had told me I couldn't meet with Christians— there were no Christians to meet with! The first few weeks were incredibly lonely; though many people were eager to see me after having been gone for so long, I no longer had relationships with them, and I craved relationships that centered around and glorified Jesus.

While my father was laying down the ground rules at home, I was learning the ground rules at my new job as well. All the teachers were coming in a month early to get started on classroom decorations, on lesson plans, and on preparing materials for our incoming students. By the time mid-August rolled around and the school year began, I had started to find my rhythm and establish relationships with the other teachers.

By this point, the cry of my heart had become for God to send other Christians to me. I desired a family who loved me because we loved Jesus, especially when my own family considered me a source of shame for that same reason. I continued to bring this before God, taking hold of his promises and believing that he would deliver what he had said. Verses like Matthew 7:7 (Ask, and it will be given to you; seek, and you will find; knock, and it will be opened to you) and Mark 11:24 (Therefore I tell you, whatever you ask in prayer, believe that you have received it, and it will be yours) became the beat of my heart, pumping hope and life into my lonely bones.

And, surprise surprise, when God makes a promise, He follows through.

## The First Family

The day God chose to let me know that He had been at work, I was leading circle time at the preschool.

"Okay kids, what song do you want to sing?" I asked, adjusting myself on my mini-stool. Nearly every hand shot up, each belonging to an enthusiastic child eager to sing their favorite song.

"Sarah, what song do you want to sing today?" I asked, choosing the little blonde girl.

"I want to sing 'Jesus Loves Me!" she said.

I fell off my chair. What? Jesus loves me? I hadn't sang that since I'd been in America! Could it be— was her family Christian? Did her parents love Jesus too?

I managed to get myself back onto the chair. "What did you say, Sarah?" I asked again, wanting to make sure that I hadn't imagined my biggest hope coming true.

"I said, 'Jesus Loves Me!" she exclaimed, "I just said that!"

"Alright class," I said, deciding to just roll with it, "One, two, three. Jesus loves me this I know. . ."

And at that moment, my boss opened up the door.

"Rebekah, you cannot sing that song here," she informed me.

"How about we sing 'Twinkle Twinkle Little Star' instead?" I asked the children, not missing a beat. "Twinkle Twinkle. . .."

After we had finished the song, I had told Sarah that I would sing 'Jesus Loves Me' with her later. When it was the last stretch of free time, I took Sarah over to a corner, and together, we sang about how much Jesus loves us.

At the end of each day, I would give a report to the parent of each child about how they did during the day. I gave each report as usual, but I was pretty much just waiting for Sarah's parents to come. Could they be the brothers and sisters I had been asking for?

"Sarah?" I heard the voice call as two parents walked into my room. I brought Sarah over to them as I quickly contemplated what to say.

"What are you?" I asked, surprising myself at my brazen choice of words. "Sarah wanted to sing 'Jesus Loves Me," I added.

"Oh," her father responded with a smile, "We are Christians!"

My jaw dropped. Though I knew that this was the only logical option, hearing someone say that they were a Christian here still rocked my world. "I-I am a Christian too!" I finally got out, the words making their way past disbelief. Husband and wife beamed.

"We are missionaries here," he said, far more quietly now, "and there are more of us.

## More of Us

The joy that meeting them filled me with that day is unexplainable. God had sent me brothers and sisters and had given me their child, not only so that I could help raise her to be the woman God intended her to be, but also because as a child, Sarah was unafraid to speak about Jesus and so alert me to other Christians in the area.

I began meeting with Sarah's family in secret and loved every moment. It brought such incredible refreshment to me to meet with others who loved Jesus, to be able to worship *with* my brothers and sisters, to do life *with* the Bride. But their words— there are more of us— kept bouncing around my mind, asking if every person I met was one of the Christians they had mentioned.

One morning, as I got my cup of coffee at the preschool, I felt my legs get hot. I had figured out by this point that my legs getting hot meant that Holy Spirit was going to do something. So I walked out of the room and down the hall to where I felt Holy Spirit leading me. On top of the door was the name of the teacher— Hope. I opened the door to find her at her desk.

"How can I help you, Rebekah?" she asked.

"I have no idea," I said, "The Holy Spirit sent me here!"

It turned out that Hope was married to a pastor, and my family had suddenly doubled in size. God was nowhere near being done.

Once more, God used his sweet children to lead me to more of his people. This time, I was playing with one of my preschoolers when he mentioned Jesus. Once again, I approached the parents to confirm where they were with Jesus, and once again, they were missionaries. It didn't take long for me to start babysitting their child in the evenings when they would be out doing ministry or having a date. Beyond just being able to have fellowship with other believers, it was my dad who would bring me there and drop me off! The very person who had said that I would never interact with Christians was the one bringing me to and from the house of Christians!

A third child soon brought a third family to my attention, and I was ecstatic. More missionaries, the wife worked with recovering addicts and had been given special permission to go into schools and talk about the program, which involved talking about Jesus! These families were my family, and we loved each other as such. They became my parents, my siblings, and their children became my children. We were truly a family.

## On the Enemy's Turf

The enemy had not forgotten that I was on his ground. Though all the Earth is God's, in my country, every person in authority worshipped Satan by worshipping Allah. And I was not content to simply sit and let my relationship with Christ die; no, I was looking to bring others to Christ as well. I was not content to sit inside a cage of fear when Jesus had already set me free. So Satan devised another plan.

It started with deprivation. One day when I was at the preschool, my mother randomly went into my closet and found my Bible, hidden and tucked away. She brought it to my father, who confronted me about it when I got home that night, and I got my first taste of persecution in action.

"Rebekah!" his voice booming, "Is this cursed book yours?"

"Yes," I answered, unwilling to lie.

"I told you 'No Bibles!' and yet, here this is! What are you thinking? That this is America?! NO, Rebekah, this is NOT America and you are forbidden to ever have a Bible again!" he raged, beginning to pace. He went on, his voice rising, but no amount of control could break the joy that Jesus had planted deep within my heart. It had already blossomed, and its sweet aroma overpowered any stench of the enemy. I was still at peace, still joyful, and especially because I knew what my father did not. Jesus was the Word. Jesus was not a book— he was in my heart. Beyond that simple fact, I already had memorized large chunks of Scripture, and no one could take those away from me. My Jesus was permanently embedded in my heart, in Spirit and in the passages that I memorized. What control the enemy grasped for, he could not have.

It was also during this time that my youngest brother, Sarmad, began dating his high school sweetheart, a woman he would later marry. This brother who would tell me within the next few months that I was his sister above all else, and no religion would get in the way of that, would soon start changing to fit into her more strictly Islamic family, a family that I defied by believing in Jesus.

# CHAPTER FOUR:
## PERSECUTION

*Come to me, all who labor and are heavy laden, and I*
*will give you rest.*
*Matthew 11:28*

## Fear and Faith

In Islam, to purge the family of the dishonor of having a blasphemer (Christian, or anyone who renounces Islam) in their family, someone from the family or community can kill the blasphemer. However, if the community feels that dishonor has infected the whole family, the whole family can be killed as well.

My family lived in fear from the moment they knew that I was a Christian. By loving Jesus, I was not only putting myself in danger, I was endangering my family.

Fear for their lives, my life, and my eternity quickly drove my family to more drastic measures. When taking away my Bible didn't stop me, they began applying intense pressure on me to return to Islam.

One clear morning, my parents and I were sitting in the living room together. The tension that had come with my profession of my faith was thick in the room, easily the cloudiest part of the day.

"So, Rebekah," my mother started, "how was. . . work, yesterday?" she asked, struggling to make conversation.

"It was goo—" my response was cut short by the piercing cry of the prayer call. The wailing notes, summoning all Muslims to pray, sang out verses from the Quran in ancient Arabic. There was a moment of stillness in the room as the prayer call drilled the room.

"Well, it's time to pray!" my father said gruffly as he got up and fumbled for his prayer mat. My family still wasn't consistent on their daily prayers, but it seemed that my father and mother would be praying today. I watched them but made no move. Instead, I began silently praying for my family's salvation.

"I said," my father spoke again, "it's time to pray." His words were stiff and forceful as his eyes darted to the open window and back, drawing those walking outside to my attention. I still made no move. I would pray to my Jesus and my Jesus alone. Baba Jee finally grasped the prayer mats and launched one in my direction. I let it thump down next to me, but made no move to pick it up.

"Baba Jee, you know I believe in Jesus. I won't do these prayers," I said in an even voice, sure of my convictions. The prayer call rang on, each note seeming to become louder than the last.

*"Rebekah!"* my father bordered on shouting as he jerked my arm up, forcing me out of my chair while throwing the prayer mat on the floor. I happened to catch a glimpse of the people in the street, who had hesitated at the sound of my father's voice. My father glanced their way too, smiled at them, and then forced me to my knees. "You will kneel, Rebekah, and you will bow as you have been taught," he whispered in my ear. "I will have no daughter of mine burning in hell and bringing shame on us."

He laid his mat out next to me and did his bows, keeping a careful eye on me the whole time. I hesitated a moment longer, but I knew the look in my father's eye, and soon I was bowing with him, empty motions to an empty god.

*Allahu Akbar. . . (God is Great)*

"Jesus, you are love."

*Allahu Akbar. . . (God is Great)*

"Jesus, *you* are love."

*Ashhadu an la ilaha illa Allah. . . (I bear witness that there is no god except the One God)*

"You are the only God, and I will worship no other, Jesus."

The prayer went on, and as the declarations of Islam were made, I instead declared who my Jesus was and my love for him. The Son of God, my Jesus, bring your people back to you. Show them your love and bring them your salvation. The forced prayers became a time for me to worship Jesus and plead for my countrymen.

"Rebekah," my father growled when the last notes had died out, "you are *my* daughter, you are in *my* house, and you *will* obey me when I tell you do to something."

"Baba Jee, you don't have to worry about people seeing me not do the prayers. Anyone seeing me isn't doing the prayers themselves, so they won't care that *I'm* not doing them! And if you're still afraid, I can just hide in my room! Or I can—"

*"Rebekah!"* he thundered. I winced and stepped back, trying to be out of range of his words and fists. He had never even threatened violence before, but things had changed while I was gone. Seeing me pull back, he sighed and turned away. "Blasted Americans," he muttered.

"What?" I asked, my courage returning the moment I was reminded of my friends across the ocean, and a protectiveness rising in me.

"Blasted. Americans."His voice grew louder, the growl returning as he turned back to me. "They brainwash you into renouncing your faith and sentencing yourself to Hell, turn you into an infidel, and then they do it so thoroughly that even when you come back, you can't see reason."

"Baba Jee—"

"No! No, Rebekah! Can't you see anything? You were healthy, you were bright— and then you go to America and get corrupted! The same year

35

you turn away from Allah, you get diagnosed with a disease! Did you think that was coincidence? Turn away from Christianity! Stop living in this lie! Stop living in the punishment of renouncing Islam! You'll get yourself and all of us killed! How foolish are you?!" he roared, raising his hands as if he wanted to strangle me before dropping them. "You will go back to your room and start thinking, and you will decide that the lies of Christianity are not worth going to Hell for," he said, his voice restrained but still threatening. I turned and walked to my room, pondering this change in my father. There was no decision to be made on going back to Islam. Abandoning my Jesus was out of the question. But my father. . . This change was alarming. He was not the man that I had left 4 years ago when I went to America, but then I was not the girl he sent. He was so angry. . . but so afraid. . . Realizing that I could do nothing to change my father, I turned to my Father in prayer, lifting up my Baba Jee and praying for his salvation.

Soon my family fell into a rhythm. I would try to hide for the daily prayers, and whether I was found and forced to do the bows or not, I would spend that time pleading for freedom for myself and my people.

## Of Church and Espionage

In November of 2000, I was approached by one of my new Christian friends while at work. There was a church they knew of, and they were having a service tonight. I immediately agreed to come with, and we made plans to leave right after the school day was over. I could hardly contain my excitement— I would be attending church! Oh to be spiritually fed again. How sweet that would be!

Finally, the day drew to a close and I happily saw my last student off. I found my friends and we quickly (but discreetly) got into her car and drove to the church. What a beautiful thing it is, to be in the presence of a family you've never met and couldn't love more, to worship alongside those who love Jesus as well, to be poured into instead constantly pouring out. Throughout the service, I was in near constant tears. Joy, acceptance, the presence of the Lord— it was all so perfect and so beautiful. None of us wanted to leave at the end of the night, and yet, that time still came. My friend drove me home, and thus ended my beautiful and happy night.

"Where have you been?" my father asked in that nonchalant tone that meant he knew something.

"At the school. I stayed late to finish up some paperwork," I said, slowly taking off my shoes.

"That's interesting. That's very interesting." He slowly stood up. "At the school, you say?"

I hesitated. "Yes. . . At the school. Where else would I be?" I drew out each word, trying to figure out what he knew and buy me time.

"Do not lie to me!" he roared, making me jump. His fingers rose to point accusingly at me. "I know where you've been. I know what you've been doing all night!" He began to pace back and forth.

"Baba Jee—"

"No! I specifically told you that you were NOT to go to church under ANY circumstances! What part of that told you that sneaking out to go to church would be good? Did you think I wouldn't find out?"

I took a step back, taking in his words.

He knew I had been to church.

But how? Had I been betrayed? Was one of the people in the congregation not a Christian? How?

"I've had people following you, Rebekah— don't try to lie to me about where you have been! I know where you go and what you do! I know who you see and when you see them! You cannot lie to me! And don't—"

I ran, the solitude of my room calling me over my father's angry voice. I was being followed? The sound of my bare feet slapping the floor followed me downstairs and into the safety of my room.

"Oh Jesus, where can I worship you? How can I love you and be with the Body if I'm being followed? And yet— and yet, Jesus— I know that this not out of your hands, and I know that you will work this for good! You are still good Jesus!"

A soft knock at the door distracted me from my prayer.

"Who is it?" I asked, my voice quiet.

"It's Sarmad," the voice of my youngest brother responded. I sighed and opened the door.

"Hey, Rebekah. I, uh, I heard what Baba Jee said," he started and then paused. "I don't care if you're a Christian," he said suddenly, the words exploding out of his mouth. "You are my sister, and I love you. No matter what, I love you." He wrapped me up in his hug before I had time to respond, but I didn't need to. I simply hugged my brother back and let all the emotions from the night come out. From the excitement and beauty of church to finding out that I was being followed, and now seeing my brother choosing love over Islam— it had been a packed night. Sarmad just held me as my tears dropped onto his shirt, as my chest heaved, as I whispered a prayer. And we know that for those who love God, *all things* work together for good. All things work together for good.

Jesus, you are good.

## Sanctuary

The year crept by, slowly, and day by day I learned how to be more secretive, how to look for people following me, to lock the door and check it different times to make sure that it was definitely locked before we even spoke the name of Jesus. I was learning to live in love instead of fear, but to walk with caution.

As time went on, the desire grew in my heart to go back to America. Day after day, I would face increasing hostility from my family and further rejection from my culture, and my heart yearned for the days of freely proclaiming the gospel to all who would listen in America. The American missionaries only amplified my desire, though they tried not to.

But as the end of the school year approached, so did the end of my contract. My boss offered to hire me for another year, but my mind had been made.

I was going to America.

The preschool had offered to take care of my visa if I went back to the U.S., but with the expectation that I would return to them a more skilled teacher, though I had no intentions of returning. I took them up on the offer, and by some miracle, I cleared it with my parents to go back to Minnesota. John's parents had opened up their home to me, and it didn't take long for me to get back on a plane and fly back to my refuge.

I was safe.

I was home.

I loved being back in America. I spent my days doing what I had done before— pouring out into ministry. I have always had a heart for evangelism, and I loved being back in a place where I could freely tell others about Jesus without fearing for my life. I had also applied for asylum, hoping to spend the rest of my days in such freedom instead of under the fear of my family.

This. This was bliss.

But not all the world had the same bliss as I.

I had come to America in the spring of 2001. I stayed there for five wonderful months, until the nation was rocked one September morning by headlines that changed everything.

*WAR ON AMERICA:*
*TWIN TOWERS AND PENTAGON ATTACKED*

It only took three weeks before I was sent back to my country. I could hardly blame Americans— they had just been horrifically attacked by Muslims, and my country was known for being Islamic and was not known for being friendly with America. And so, my five months of bliss came to a sudden and painful close.

Coming home brought with it a surprising amount of shame for me. I felt like the runaway child being brought home by a watchful neighbor: embarrassed, ashamed, and waiting for the punishment of my parents. That whole first week, my father had no idea how to react. Sometimes he was angry and shouting obscenities at me for leaving. Sometimes he was quiet as he took in the gravity of what had taken place. Sometimes he acted like I had never left.

Sarmad, my youngest brother, had changed while I was gone. It was a subtle shift at first, a deliberate distance he kept between us that I assumed was because I had left for five months. I knew that he had started dating a girl over the summer, a girl from a devout Muslim family, but I was confident in what he had told me nearly a year ago: that I was his sister above all else.

I spent a lot of time in prayer that week; asking God to send me back, pleading with him to let me be the "terrorist" who shows them love, to give me refuge back in America again. But after a few days, a conviction began to grow in my heart. I had left not because Jesus wanted me to leave, but because I wanted to escape and hadn't trusted God to get me out in his timing. I had to wrestle that out with God for almost a week before I was willing to admit that I hadn't been willing to trust God to do what was best for me, and I repented.

"Rebekah," I heard him saying one night as I prayed, "My will is not only perfect and what is best, it is what is best *for you*. I have only good things planned for you. They will come in hard packages sometimes, but the gift is always worth it. Just because America seemed better because it was safe doesn't mean that it was best. Ask me first, Rebekah, and choose what is best, not what seems good."

## Step By Step

Five months after I had come home and repented, it seemed to occur to me and my parents at the same time that I was now jobless. Not only had I turned down the offer of another year at the preschool, but after 9/11, all Americans were brought home. The international school was

42

currently shut down, and all the missionaries were gone.

Beyond having nothing to do all day, suddenly I had lost all my friends, my prayer warriors, and my Family. I was alone. And being home all day every day meant that I was being shown more and more hostility. I started spending more and more time in prayer in my room, withdrawing from my family as best I could, but it was to no avail.

Soon it wasn't just me that was sick of me being home. My father approached me one night with one of the best questions I had ever been asked (right after "Will you say grace?").

"Rebekah, what do you want to do?" he asked. Fortunately, this time I had already prayed about it and caught God's dream for me, which had become my dream too.

"I want to have my own preschool," I answered, wondering if he would just help me find a job at a different preschool.

"Alright. Where do you want it?" he asked. I paused, taken aback. He was actually going to help me have my own preschool? He was an architect, so I supposed it didn't seem so far out of the question for him, but this was not the response I was expecting.

Still, he had meant it, and we spent the next year building my preschool. My father named it "Step By Step," and helped with all the advertising. I watched in awe as God brought my dream to life with each raised wall, with each stroke of a paintbrush bringing color into my classrooms. What a miracle this preschool was!

We spent nearly eight months in relative harmony as we worked toward a common goal together. It was by no means perfect between my father and I, and he still didn't trust me at all, but that was some of the best time I had spent with him since I became a Christian. Those are still some of the most precious memories I have with him.

Soon the preschool was built, and all the paperwork was being finished. It was time to staff my school. We had dozens of applications to go through, so we weeded out the ones that we could clearly see that we didn't want and then held the interviews. It took two full days of interviews to get through everyone, and then we still had to go back and decide who we wanted. As we dug through all the applications and tried to keep track of what face belonged to what name, there was one woman who stuck out to me and who I couldn't get out of my mind. I prayed about the position, I prayed about her, and then I just prayed some more, and after spending more time looking and discussing applications, I had made up my mind: I wanted to hire Alia.

"How did you know she was a Christian?" my father said angrily when I told him my decision.

"She's a Christian?" I asked, stunned and excited. No wonder God had chosen her!

I prayed about it for a week, making sure this time that my heart was set on God, not what I wanted. When I was confident that this was God, not me, I told my father my decision.

My father mulled over it for a few days, but God was already working on his heart.

We hired her the next week.

## Almost Dead

Now, all that was left to do was the last few touch ups and continue advertising to get more students. It was now the summer of 2002, and it was a wickedly hot summer. Beyond that, there was an electricity shortage. To keep from dying of heat, we all slept in my parents bedroom and then blasted the air conditioning all night. My family did this for about a week, and fell into that routine, and it all was well. In fact, this wouldn't have been notable at all, until the night that I woke up.

I woke up in the middle of the night, and I still don't know what woke me up, but as my eyes opened that tiny slice, I could see my father standing over me. His lips were trembling, his eyes would open up and then shut tightly. He looks like he was on the verge of tears, and I wasn't sure why it first until the glint of metal came into my line of sight.

My father had a sword raised over his head.

A sword raised over me.

My father was contemplating whether or not to kill me.

I froze, my eyes quickly closing again as I pretended that I was still asleep. Could I plead with him? Would that convince him to let me live, or be the final push for him to bring down the store? Was this my time to die? Dear Jesus, please help me. Keep me alive if you want me here on Earth, or make it quick if it's time for me to be with you in heaven.

To live is Christ, to die is gain.

To live is *Christ*, to die is *gain*.

To *live* is *Christ*.

To die *is* gain.

I continue to lay there, still, but I was becoming more and more focused on my heavenly Father than on my earthly one.

Jesus, I believe your truth.

To live is Christ, to die is gain.

Jesus I believe this. And if this means that I die right now, then to die *is* gain. I felt a bubble of peace start rising.

I believe your promises. I believe that what you say is true. I believe that you are able to stop this sword or to make this quick and painless.

To live is Christ. To die is gain.

I can do all things through Christ who strengthens me. Christ, strengthen me. Give me the peace that surpasses all understanding.

The bubble of peace seemed to have grown and burst all over me. I breathed deeply, free in the knowledge that nothing bad could happen right now. There was no need to fear. This was a win-win situation.

Confident in my Jesus, I opened my eyes again, just enough to see the empty place where my father had previously stood. I had been so focused on Jesus that I didn't notice when the danger passed. He was gone.

So I simply smiled and fell back asleep.

## CHAPTER FIVE:
## THE LIGHT SHINES IN THE DARKEST NIGHT

*I can do all things through Christ who strengthens me.*
*Philippians 4:13*

### Wrong Truth, Right Heart

"Rebekah," my mother asked one winter afternoon in 2003, "how did they get you to become a Christian in America?"

The words practically bubbled out of my mouth as I gleefully recounted that day 5 years ago when I accepted Jesus at Evelyn's house. Mama was asking about how I became a Christian? Oh Jesus, use this! Speak the same truth to her that you spoke to me!

"So. . ." Mama said when I had finished, "they brainwashed you into becoming a Christian by reading you the Bible?"

My heart sank. This was what she had heard me saying? She had missed the whole point. . .

"Mama, you didn't hear me. It wasn't that they read me the Bible, it's that Jesus is alive and he captured my heart. Hearing the Bible was a part of it, but it was the truth of who Jesus is that convinced me to choose him."

My mother nodded, but I knew that look on her face. She had heard what she wanted to hear, and whatever I said now would probably be ignored. So I spent the next few days praying for her and asking Holy Spirit to use the truth that I had shared with her to change her heart and bring her to Jesus, but she spent the next few days making a different plan.

Just four days later, a Mullah (the Muslim equivalent of a pastor) showed up at our front door. My mother greeted him excitedly while I stood off to the side, confused as to why he was there.

"Thank you so much for coming," my mother said, "I'm so glad that you could make it."

"Of course," he replied, "anything it takes to bring someone back to Allah."

I was still confused, but I was catching on. The Mullah was there for me.

"Rebekah," my mother said as she turned to me, "go wait in the living room while we get set up."

I was unsure of what to do. I knew that whatever they were doing, I was not going to like it, but I was unsure of how to honor my parents and Jesus. So I turned and started walking towards the living room, but I was far more focused on my prayer then I was on where I was walking.

Jesus, whatever happens, I choose you. Don't let me turn away from you. Don't let me dishonor you, and don't let me step out of line. Let me show them your love, Jesus, let them experience your incredible love and grace through me today. Let the day that they try to bring me back to Islam be the day that you bring them to yourself instead.

So I sat in the living room and waited, continuing to pray.

Jesus, remind me of your truth. Bring me back to when you first captured my heart, and let me share the truth with them that you shared with me that day.

Soon, I was joined by my mother and the Mullah.

"Remember, Rebekah," my mother said in an almost scolding tone, "you must stay and listen. Honor your elders. You will remember the truth that you knew once before." She gave me one more pointed look before Mama turned and began walking back to the kitchen.

The Mullah got down on his prayer mat and prayed to Allah, that Allah would be victorious this day and take back the people he deserves. Then the Mullah got up, and told me that in no time, I would be back to my old self. And with that, he opened up the Quran and started reading. The moment he began to read, I impulsively started whispering scripture to myself.

Hebrews 13:8 Jesus Christ is the same yesterday and today and forever.

Philippians 4:13 I can do all things through him who strengthens me.

Isaiah 41:10 Fear not, for I am with you; be not dismayed, for I am your God; I will strengthen you, I will help you, I will uphold you with my righteous right hand.

Soon, I was repeating every verse I knew and then starting over again. He stayed for one hour that day, just reading the Quran. I was exhausted when he left; though I had simply been sitting for an hour, I had been doing warfare for an hour. As soon as he was out the door, I was on my way to my room, hoping to counter all the lies that had just been read to me by reading the Truth. My mother caught me on my way up, though, wanting to talk to me.

"So, how was it?

"Mama, you know I don't believe what he was telling me," I said.

"Rebekah," my mother said in an unusual outburst, "you have to come back to truth. None of us want to see you going to hell over something like this!" I could see tears in my mother's eyes. "Just come back to Islam! Do your prayers! Worship Allah! You don't have to put yourself through this, and make life more difficult for yourself and everyone else! We just want to see you go to heaven!"

"But Mama," I said, "I am going to heaven. You guys are right, Christianity is very different than Islam, but Christianity is the reason I know I'm going to heaven. The truth that Jesus is alive is the best assurance anyone could give me that I am going to heaven." I paused for a moment, then decided to continue. "In fact, Mama, I'm worried about you going to heaven. Jesus is the only way. Allah won't give a guarantee of salvation, even if you are a Muslim your whole life, but Jesus can promise eternal life because it isn't dependent on what we do but on him— and he loves us!"

But Mama just sighed and walked away, dismissing me and my words.

For the next four months, the Mullah came in every day and read the Quran to me. Every day, I would be exhausted, but every day, I became more and more familiar with my Bible.

## Big Brother

Two more years passed. The preschool was doing well, though the first year had been exhausting. Alia was amazing, and I loved working with her every day. We would often use the time after school when everyone assumed we were cleaning and preparing for tomorrow to worship and pray together. After triple checking the locks and shades, we would whisper our prayers together and let Holy Spirit flood the room. Often, as we were praying, I would hear the song "Old Rugged Cross" playing so clearly that I would have to go check the radio to make sure it was actually off! Not long after that, Alia would usually hear it as well, and we would thank Jesus for providing music to worship to, even when no physical instruments were present.

It was such an encouragement to have Alia walking with me during those times, especially when the spring of 2005 came. My father received a summons from the government, and though that was noteworthy, it didn't initially cause us concern. It wasn't until my father came home that night, wearied and fearful, that we began to take it seriously.

"Rebekah," he said as he practically fell onto the couch, "it was about you."

Fear flashed through my body. "Me?"

"Yes, you. Did you think you could speak so boldly about Christianity and not be noticed?" He paused for a moment, his head in his hands. "You've been accused of blasphemy."

My whole family froze.

"Blasphemy?" my mother asked, clearly shaken.

"Yes, blasphemy. They've been reading your emails, Rebekah. They had them all printed out and laid in front of me. They wanted to throw you in jail."

I didn't move as the news washed over me.
Blasphemy.
Spying.
Jail.
The whole room was silent.

Emails.

Friends.

Exposed.

*Jail.*

"What did you do?" Mama finally asked, shaking everyone out of our silent stupors.

"I told them that Rebekah was not in her senses and would never intentionally blaspheme the Prophet and the Conversion."

"But she did," Sarmad piped in. Baba Jee threw a deadly glare his way and silenced my brother.

"I convinced them not to throw her in jail, Sarmad. Would you rather have your sister imprisoned for this foolishness?"

"So they aren't doing anything about it?" Mama asked, a hint of hopefulness in her voice.

"They've marked her passport so that she can't leave the country. She can't even ride in anything that could get her out of the country. No planes, boats, trains, or cars."

Mama breathed a sigh of relief. "Well, it's not good, but it's better than jail."

"Do you see what you've done?" Sarmad snapped. "You almost got put in jail, and you made Baba Jee *lie* to keep you out! How selfish are you? You're putting the whole family in danger and you know it! Just give it up! Jesus isn't worth it— and if he was really real, if he was as loving as you say, then he wouldn't put everyone else in danger! It's one thing to condemn yourself but don't drag the rest of the family down with you!"

"Sarmad, you know I'm not trying to get you in trouble, and they weren't after you guys, they were after me! And Jesus—"

"Stop it! Stop defending blasphemy! Stop cursing Allah with every breath you take!" Sarmad was shouting now, his hands alternating between clenched fists and accusing fingers. "Stop bringing shame on *us* so that *you* can be happy! Come back to Islam and let this stupidity go!"

"Enough! It is finished," Baba Jee said, silencing the room once more with his voice. "It is already over, no need to torment your sister more, Sarmad."

Sarmad continued to hold my gaze, his fury barely contained. Wasn't this the brother who told me that I was his sister above all? Oh Jesus, Jesus. . .

I finally just shut my eyes so I wouldn't have to see Sarmad's drilling into me. It was then that I noticed that my cheeks were soaked and my eyes had the salty burn of tears. I had no idea when I had started crying, but that was all I wanted to do right now.

After another few moments of silence, I heard the soft tapping of Mama leaving the room, and I followed suite, going down to my room.

Jesus, I don't know how much more of this I can take. They don't see your love, they see selfishness. Show them your truth, Jesus.

Show them your truth.

## CHAPTER SIX:
## THE MOSQUE

*When I am afraid, I put my trust in you.*
Psalm 56:3

### Lydia

It was now February of 2009, and the numbers in my preschool had peaked and now were plummeting. We had started with 10, and slowly gained numbers until we had 26 students in my school. But then, the students started leaving. Some left at the end of the year, some got pulled out in the middle of the year. It wasn't until years later that my father told me why— that parents were getting upset that their children were learning to sing Jesus songs at my preschool. I now only had three students left: Amin (Faith), Ayse (Peace), and Barakat (Blessing). I took their names as a sign that God was still with me in the preschool.

One afternoon, my father and I were invited to a picnic by a family friend. As everyone ate lunch together, I noticed the daughter of the friend, Lydia, sitting under a tree. I knew that look on her face; it was more than loneliness— she was alone. It was like I was looking at myself during the first few years of college. Surrounded by strangers who I should know but don't. A whole world of potential friends, but not a single one to call my own. I needed to talk to Lydia as much as I had needed someone to talk to me.

"Isn't the air so fresh here? Look at how beautiful God made these mountains," I said as I sat down next to her, "all the birds, the flowers, the butterflies— they're stunning!"

Lydia smiled at me and we began talking. I remembered how desperately I had needed Jesus, the promise and hope of being loved perfectly and wholly, and so I used nature to describe how Jesus talks to us, and that he talks to us because he loves us. We talked for around ten minutes before my father told me it was time to leave, so I gave her the hug I knew she needed and then we left.

My life went on, and I went back to teaching and my normal life. I didn't even think about Lydia again until over a week later, when Holy Spirit brought Lydia to mind. After praying about her for a while, I decided to ask my father if he knew anything about her.

"Lydia?" If his voice didn't make it clear enough, his face did. My question had taken him aback.

"Yeah. Is it weird that I brought her up?"

"Well, not normally, but I just talked to her parents today. . . She has been acting out ever since the picnic, and that's not like her. She's been swearing at her parents, throwing things in the house— the poor girl just snapped. They're taking her to a Mullah tonight to figure out what's going on."

"What? What happened? Why is she doing this?"

My father gave me a pointed look for a moment before answering. "You tell me, Rebekah. You were the last one to talk to her before she lost it."

I decided it would be best not to say anything more and instead went back to my room, praying for Lydia all the way.

Jesus, be with her. . . Let her hold onto your truth and not lose it. Keep her in your hands. . .

I continued to pray for her as the next day came and went, and the day after as well. I was waiting for news, but I wasn't sure what kind of news I was hoping for. Certainly not that Lydia would stop acting out by following Islam more closely. But how would I know if she had chosen Jesus? They wouldn't let her leave the mosque if she became a Christian. . . Oh Jesus. . . Help her. . .

And then, one evening my answer came. I walked upstairs from my room and found my father sitting on the couch with his head in his hands, my mother by his side. They were whispering back and forth, but as soon as my mother noticed me, they stopped.

"Is everything alright?" I asked.

"Rebekah, we just heard back about Lydia," my mother said, pausing for a moment as she looked at my dad.

"They beat an evil spirit out of her with a broom, but the spirit said that it came from you. The Mullah wants you to come in."

"No! I'm not going in somewhere where they beat the devil out of you with a broom! Besides, I don't have a demon— I have Jesus! He is as far away from a demon as you can get!"

My parents looked at each other for a moment, and then my father got up to leave.

"Baba Jee, don't make me do this," I pleaded, "it's not right!"

But my father was already out the door.

**They Will Persecute You Also. . .**

Mere days had passed since I had heard the news about Lydia, but my mind was far from the threat of the mosque. It was lunchtime at the preschool, and I was having a grand time with Alia.

We were watching the students play as we sipped our coffee, and lunch with Alia was always good for my soul. It was nearing the end of lunch, however, and we would soon have to leave the small tables we sat at. But as I got ready to go back, I noticed two figures approaching: Baba Jee and Vashti— a family friend who had taught me the Quran as a child.

Something was wrong.

Very wrong.

Baba Jee and Vashti coming to my preschool was certainly strange, but there was something else wrong about the situation, and I wasn't sure what it was.

My muscles began to tighten as I waited for one of them to speak. I exchanged glances with Alia, but the look on her face made it clear that she had no explanation either.

No one said a word as they approached, but Vashti and Baba Jee both picked up the pace. I kept trying to make eye contact with my father, but he might as well have been a masked soldier for all the expression his face held.

There was a moment of tense uncertainty as they reached the table, but it quickly melted away into fear.

"COME!" Vashti practically shouted as they each grabbed one of my arms, their fingers too tight on my skin.

"I- I have students!" I said, jerking my elbows back uselessly to get free.

"You don't have any students!" Vashti retorted as she and my father forced me out of my chair and started bringing towards the van parked on the street.

Pure terror ripped through my body, clearing my mind of any sane thoughts and my body of any mobility. I half walked, half skipped, half dragged my feet along as they kept moving toward the street. My mind would have been racing had it not been lost on the treadmill of fear, keeping the same three thoughts in my head.

What is happening?

Where are they taking me?

They're going to hurt me.

As we neared the van, I realized my legs were uncomfortably warm and moist.

"I-I wet my pants. I have to go home," I said, the words coming out slowly as though I was just learning how to speak my native language. There was a moment of hesitation as they exchanged glances, but they said nothing as they pushed me into the car.

Get out.

Open the door.

Leave.

Pound on the windows.

Scream.

Grab the steering wheel.

My brain was full of ideas on how to get out, but my body was refusing to listen to anything it said. I sat motionless in the seat, unable to even move my eyes from the front windshield as I watched the drive back to my house.

Baba Jee opened the door and jerked my out of the car by my arm. I stumbled out, and he mostly drug me into the house, but let me go by myself into my room.

I changed slowly, putting on new pants and grabbing my American Eagle sweatshirt that I loved so much. It took me four tries to get it tied around my waist; between my shaking and the lack of communication from my brain, my hands didn't know what to do.

I began the trek back to the door, unsure of why I was going, unsure of what else to do. The small time spent in my room had calmed me enough to let me walk undeterred, even if my hands were still useless. Baba Jee wasn't waiting at the door like I had expected, and though my brain was telling me to run anywhere else, my legs were deaf to the message and kept going out to the car. Once I stepped out into the sunlight, in the momentary pause of being blinded, hands locked onto my arms again and started pulling me back to the car. The small relief I had had in my room all vanished as my whole body locked up and my brain felt like it ran into a wall. I was watching everything happening, but my brain couldn't keep up with it enough to even come up with coherent thoughts, much less tell my body to do something. As we got closer to the car, the overwhelming fear somehow increased and my brain shut off.

When I came to, just moments later, my head was underneath the car. Had I fallen?

As soon as that thought entered my mind, it was pushed out by my body letting me know that it didn't like being dragged on the concrete. Two men I didn't recognize were pulling me out and up, and then put me back in the car, next to Baba Jee. I looked at him confusion for a moment, but he just shook his head and moved me onto the floor.

I felt the car moving, and occasionally I was swung to one side or another as we took turns, but my mind was in park with the emergency brake on and it had no intentions of moving anytime soon.

Soon I was getting pulled out of the car again, and dragged into another building. But wait— was it a building? No— there were so many stairs!

We were on the Titanic!

"Are we going into the Titanic?" I asked Baba Jee. He didn't respond, so I asked again.

"Are we going into the Titanic?"

More silence. But no— we must be on the Titanic!

"I can't believe we're going on the Titanic— it's so big!"

"Is this the Titanic?"

"When is the Titanic leaving?"

"Do I have my tickets?"

"Do you hear her? She lost it. She's crazy," I heard Vashti say, but I couldn't get over the fact that I was on the Titanic. What an incredible experience!

Eventually, we came to a doorway and took off our slippers. An Imam was sitting inside, as well as Mama. Somewhere in my mind, the thought to greet them occurred, but it never made it to the forefront of my mind, much less actually leave my lips.

Baba Jee and Vashti had not stopped, however, and took me directly to the couch. I sank in, reveling in how comfortable it was and forgetting the stress of the situation for a moment. Words were exchanged between the other people in the room, but I was lost in my couch. My couch on the Titanic. How lovely.

I stared at my mother in complete satisfaction with my couch while she looked back in confusion and began to unfold a piece of cloth. I had no cares about what she would do with it or why she had it— it was simply a cloth. Then she began wrapping my head up in a hijab, and I knew that something was wrong with that, but I couldn't quite figure out what it was or why I needed to resist, much less how.

When headphones were suddenly over my ears, I realized I should probably figure out what was going on, but my brain was still moving slowly and I was having trouble getting my bearings. Then the Quran started blasting through the headphones, and a switch flipped in me.

I can do *all* things through Christ who strengthens me.

I can do all things through *Christ* who strengthens me.

I can do all things through Christ who *strengthens* me.

My mini chant went on, the truth stirring in my heart. My ears had tuned out the hum of the Quran the moment it began to play, for this was a far more important melody.

*I* can do all things through Christ who strengthens me.

I can do all things *through* Christ who strengthens me.

I can do all things through Christ who strengthens *me*.

The Quran played out for 15 minutes, but I didn't hear a word of it. I was busy with Truth. But the Mullah had no idea of that as he took the headphones off and held my gaze for a few seconds too long.

"I will help you," he said emphatically.

Part of my brain had turned back on, and knew that he meant what he said, but that what he meant was not going to actually help me because we had very different end goals.

My body instinctively tensed at the sight of the broom that he was now pulling out. "Here comes the beating. . ." I thought as images of Lydia flooded back into my mind. I closed my eyes as he raised it, whispering a prayer. . .

. . . But the blow never came. When a light tap came on my shoulder, I opened my eyes in surprise; he was now moving the broom to the other shoulder, as if he was knighting me. I watched in confusion as he tapped each shoulder, going back and forth. Was this it? Was this the beating I was worried about?

It didn't last long, though, and he soon sent me into another room. Mama and Baba Jee did not follow— but I was certainly not alone in this room.

I was surrounded by people, none of whom I knew. One of them closed the door behind me while another pushed a chair toward me. I sat, hoping that this would be as painless as the other.

Suddenly my head was being pulled backwards, so that my face was parallel with the ceiling. My eyes went wild trying to find who was holding me back, but the rest of my body seemed disconnected again and wouldn't move. Then a Mullah came back into my line of sight with a small vial of black liquid.

"I'm going to put some of this black liquid in your eyes. Tell me what you see," his voice far more foreboding than the Mullah before. Hands reached out and held open my eyelids.

I watched him pull out a large dropper and hold it over my eyes for a moment.

Jesus help me.

The drop of black fell, splashing into my left eye. Burning followed the blackness that now covered my eye as a wail forced its way out of my throat. While my left eye was still being scorched and blinded, another drop landed in my right eye. Darkness filled my vision and both of my eyes now screamed in pain. But the drops kept coming. Left, right, left, right— each drop bringing a new wave of burning.

Jesus, help me!

Suddenly, a cross blazed through the blackness covering my eyes.

"What do you see?" I heard the Mullah ask.

"I see the cross of my Jesus!" I exclaimed, clinging to this hope.

"Close your eyes and try again," he said, and the hands let go of my face. I blinked a few times, but the cross would not leave.

"Well, what color is it?" he asked, clearly becoming frustrated.

"It's white. . . now pink. . . now it's changing colors!" I exclaimed, focusing on the cross over the pain now.

Suddenly a hand gripped my arm too tightly and an unfamiliar voice spoke: "Say the Muslim prayer of faith."

Trembling, I did as he asked, the cross still in my sights. Jesus, my heart is not in this.

"Again." And I did.

"Again." Once more, I did. But as the words finished coming out of my mouth, I felt something harden in me. I would not forsake my lover. I would not forsake my Jesus. Like Peter and the rooster's crow, I was done abandoning my God.

"Again."

"No."

"I said again!"

"No!"

I heard the voice grunting in frustration for a moment before I heard a clicking noise, and then smoke drifted into my nostrils.

"I said again!" the voice shouted.

"No!" I yelled back.

Suddenly, pain tore up my nose as a piece of burning paper was pushed up as far as it could go. I screamed and tried to take it out, but someone was holding my hands back. My whole chest clenched up and I wanted my nose to fall off if it would just hurt less.

"I can do all things through Christ who strengthens me!" I shouted, praying that Jesus would take away the pain. I squeezed my eyes closed tighter one more time before blowing as hard as I could out of my nose as I opened my eyes.

"Jesus," I whispered. Most of the paper had come out of my nose, and not only that, but my eyes were clear now. "I can see!"

"Ears, next," I heard a man say, their voice tight.

"No, no, no no no nonono please don't! Please, please don't!" I yelled as I heard the same click of a lighter. "Jesus! Jesus! Help me!"

The jolt of my eardrum getting hit was soon replaced by my ear burning. It felt like it was in my brain, like my whole mind was going to catch on fire and go up into a smoking heap. And then the same jolt came into my other ear. My whole body started convulsing, trying to get the pain out of my ears. I ripped one of my arms free and grabbed my ear, but I couldn't reach the fire. It continued to burn, and I continued to scream as my arm was recaptured and pinned down again.

"I CAN DO ALL THINGS THROUGH CHRIST WHO STRENGTHENS ME!" The shriek tore its way out of my throat, and for a moment everything was still and nothing hurt in its wake. But then the moment ended and the pain was angry it had been silenced.

"NO!" I heard someone roar, and then someone was grabbing my jaw and forcing it open. I tried yanking my head back, but it was already tilted too far and I couldn't bring it back anymore. I heard the clicking once more, and smoke was just starting to reach my one good nostril, when suddenly my tongue was being scorched.

I screamed again, trying to shake loose, trying to cough it out, but I couldn't. Then it was being shoved further back, further down my throat. My whole mouth turned dry and my lungs started panicking when all they got was smoke. I started coughing more, but the burning wouldn't leave. I felt like I was suffocating, choking on the smoke that was both coming out of my mouth and going into my lungs.

My throat and ears and nose continued to burn, but the room was shifting now. I could see people moving through the tears in my eyes and focused on that to distract from the pain.

"Is the fire out?" a man asked.

"Just about," another responded.

"Move her as soon as it's out," the first voice said, and then there was silence again.

As the fire died out in my ears, nose, and throat, the pain did not. I was still coughing up ash and could feel the blisters still rising in my ears when I was dragged through another doorway.

There were a few people in this room. A younger Mullah that I didn't recognize, a few other men, and Vashti. I was dropped on the floor, and Vashti came over and held my neck, as though she wanted to support my head.

"How can I help you?": he asked, his eyebrows furrowed as he kept looking back and forth between my eyes, studying me.

No.

Just no.

How can he ask that as if he cares after I was just tortured?

I was just tortured.

*Tortured.*

And now he wants to act like he cares.

How dare he.

How *dare* he.

How dare all of them?

And without further thought, just the whirling rage driving me, I leaned forward.

And I spit in his face.

## The Breaking Point

There was a moment where everything was still. A stillness that let me have a moment to realize that spitting in his face was the worst possible thing I could have done. A stillness where I felt God's presence all around me, thick in the room like butter. A stillness that let him watch my spit come flying at his face and decide what he was going to do afterwards.

And then the stillness was over.

His hands went two different directions—one up to wipe off his face and the other one down towards his feet. I only had a moment to wonder before his hand came back up with his slipper in it and he was winding up to hit me with it. I cringed in anticipation, but the rubber sole was already slamming into my chest, knocking all the air out of my lungs.

"JESUS!" I heard myself say as all the air came whooshing out.

The slipper came again,

"JESUS!"

My lungs couldn't get enough air in fast enough.

"JESUS!"

Again and again and again, the slipper pounded my chest, leaving it stinging and empty, searching for the air it needed. And every time, the only word I could say was "Jesus."

I heard the man cussing and muttering to himself for a moment, and then there were no more blows. I took in as many deep breaths as I could, trying to get my lungs back to normal, but then suddenly water came in with the air. I sputtered for a moment, but the water kept coming. I rolled over, using that moment to grab some more air and see what was going on.

It was a spray bottle.

Part of me wanted to laugh. A spray bottle? That's it? It doesn't even hurt!

But he had not stopped spraying me while I was thinking. At first it didn't seem like a big deal— but as my face started dripping and my shirt started to get soaked, I became more and more uncomfortable. It certainly wasn't physically painful, but pain wasn't the point. I felt like a cat that he was trying to get off the table, or a car that he was going to wash.

The torture before had been inhumane, but this was the first time that I felt like less than human.

The mind games, the blistering ears, the dripping nose, the aching eyes— I starting losing it. I starting panting— Jesus— Jesus— Jesus— his name coming out between breaths. Where are you Jesus? *Where are you?* Are you coming? Can't you see I'm not okay? Can't you see I need help? Are you actually going to do something about this?

Where are you?

And then I was being lifted up. There were no ropes, no chains, no medieval torture devices. Just hands— so many hands all over my body— stretching my body out so that I was facing the ceiling.

"Jesus," I whispered once more as I shut my eyes.

And then, I was in a chair. What? My eyes popped open again, investigating my surroundings. Vashti was whispering something into the Mullah's ears, and then he nodded and left, motioning for the others to leave with him. It was just Vashti and I now.

"Rebekah, are you a virgin?" she asked. My mind flashed back to John.

"I don't know what you mean," I answered, trying to push all those nights with John out of my head.

"You know what I mean. Are you a virgin?"

"I—" I stopped, unsure of what to say.

"Your mother already told me about the American man. Are you a virgin?" she asked once more.

This time I didn't even bother answering. She already knew. What did this mean? I just stared at Vashti for a little bit until she sighed and got up. I watched blankly as she walked over to the door and whispered some more to the men outside. And then they came pouring back in, a fire in their eyes that hadn't been there before. The Mullah reached out, looking like he was going to grab me, but instead I slammed into the marble floor— the breath leaving my lungs again. I gasped for air, trying to breath again, trying to ignore all the bones in my back that were screaming at me. I curled up on my side, my eyes squeezed shut, as I felt hands grab me again. I was dragged across the floor, any exposed skin catching and pulling and scraping. I was brought through another doorway, and then someone was grabbing my pants as the door closed. Suddenly, I was naked and exposed.

And then I was raped.

I don't know how long I was in the room. I don't know how many men were there. I don't know how many times I screamed or begged them to stop or cried out to Jesus. But at some point, my pants came back on. At some point, I was brought back out to the other room. At some point, I was left on the floor. And at some point, I blacked out.

**Going Home**

The lights were too bright.

The floor was too cold.

My whole body ached.

My ears felt like they were still on fire.

Tears were pouring over my cheeks.

But now someone was speaking.

". . . up. We need to go. We can get help, but first you have to get up." Alia? Why was she here?

"Rebekah. Get up." She sounded frustrated. How long had she been there?

I closed my eyes again, wanting to return to the bliss of the unconscious world, where nothing hurt.

Why did it hurt?

Black drops. Fire. Chest. Water. Naked.

The memories jolted through my body like electricity, and I curled up on my side, sobs and wails clashing as they fought for my breath. No, no, this couldn't have happened. No, not this. Not all this.

At some point, Alia's hand was on my shoulder, as first reassuring, gently rubbing. But then it turned into shaking, and I started to hear her speak through my wails.

"Rebekah. We need to go. Stop crying or I'm going to leave. You are okay now. We need to go."

The only thing worse than not crying would have been being alone again, so I fought back the sobs and cut short my screaming. I let her help me up, though my body didn't want to move at all, and she half-led-half-carried me out to her car.

There was driving, and questions, and holding my hand. A hospital, and nurses with more questions. My parents. My brothers. "She's depressed." More questions. White coats, a bed that crinkled, and someone helping me into a gown. IV's. Antidepressants. Questions.

But my mind had plunged off the path of sanity and dove into the underbrush and woods, hoping to find some reality where nothing that had just happened was real.

And then I was home.

## The Reality I Lost

Lydia had returned to normal after her visit to the mosque, I was told.

I did not.

The lights were watching me. I just knew it. There were cameras in the lights so the lights needed to be off. Turn the lights off. Leave them off. NOW.

My bed. I can't leave. Not for another 3 weeks. Well then I just won't eat. No— no the food is feces. Stop trying to feed it to me.

I can't go to the bathroom. There are lights I can't turn off.

They'll find me.

Phone calls under blankets. Don't make me eat the feces. Tell them to stop.

Pain.

Pain like needles, all over my body. It was needles. It was acupuncture.

"No, you never had acupuncture, Rebekah."

Little pin pricks everywhere. Never stopping. Always hurting.

3 am. All the lights must be on. Flick. Flick. Flick. Living room. Hallway. Kitchen. Look out the window. There's a cross from the light. Look, Mom.

"There's no cross, but there is a wedding out there. Look, Rebekah."

No wedding. Just a cross. The cross is gone.

PCA's. Strange woman, here for hours. Making me eat. Making me drink. Giving me pills. Cleaning. Go to the bathroom. Come with me.

School? No school. Bed. Stay in bed. But not with lights on. Bad lights. Lights out.

For a month, I refused to eat because I thought that it was actually feces, and I hated the lights because I thought there were cameras in them. I was suspicious of everyone, hated everyone, and was delusional. It was only after I had been through four weeks of a complete break with reality that I started to get better.

I began eating again. I stopped taking the medication. I taught myself to ignore the lights until I forgot about them. I picked up my Bible again and ran through the familiar pages, absorbing the truth that had been so absent.

Eventually, I came back to the school and continued to teach. Eventually, my life returned to normal. Eventually, I learned how to not think about what had happened.

# CHAPTER SEVEN:
# FASTING AND PRAYER

*He must increase, but I must decrease.*
*John 3:30*

## Curses and Fasts

A few years went by, and it was now 2012. I had suffered from severe acne all over my body for years, and both my family and I were reaching our breaking points. My mother brought me into the hospital, to dermatologists, and many different doctors to get treatment. But with every medication, it only got worse. Finally, one of my Christian friends approached me and simply said, "Rebekah, stop going to doctors. The problem is spiritual, not physical." She gave me the number of her pastor, and that was the end of the conversation.

I reached out to Pastor Seif that same day, but it didn't go well. We'd go back and forth in conversation, but we couldn't understand each other. The phone kept breaking up, our voices were distorted, and it often sounded like we were speaking different languages.

It took a few days, but eventually we did get to talk to each other. After explaining the situation, we prayed about it for a little while and Holy Spirit told Pastor Seif that someone had put a black magic spell on me.

"So Rebekah," he continued, "I really think you should fast and pray for three days, and Jesus will tell you who it was that cursed you."

"Pastor Seif, I don't want to know who cursed me! I don't want to hold a grudge against them or hate them!" I responded, genuinely concerned about who it was that would have cursed me.

"Matthew 5:44. Do you remember that verse?" He paused for a moment to let me think before continuing on. "'Love your enemies, and pray for those who persecute you.' How can you pray for people you don't know? Rebekah, I don't want you to hate anyone either, but I would rather you know who it was, forgive them, and be able to pray specifically for them than question everyone in your life forever."

I finally agreed, and we made a plan. For three days in a row, I would fast from midnight until five o'clock the next evening. And just like Seif said, every day, I would get a name.

My grandma's servant, my aunt, and a local widow ended up being the three names I got. Each day, when I would hear a name, I would send it to the pastor, and he would confirm that he had heard the same thing. I would spend the rest of the day forgiving and praying for that person, and by the end of the third day, I was completely healed! No more acne, no more scars, nothing! All of it was gone!

For the first time, I was really experiencing the power of a fast, and how it heightened all your senses to where and how Jesus is moving.

## Rebekah the Prophet

Not long after that, I had a deep longing to have the gift of prophecy. I talked to Pastor Seif about it, and he confirmed that he had been praying for me to receive the gift of prophecy as well.

"So, what do I do now?" I asked him.

"Well, now it's time to listen closely to Holy Spirit, and do whatever he tells you, even if it means doing something that seems to have nothing to do with prophecy."

"How will I know?"

"Rebekah," he said, giving me one of those you-just-asked-a-question-you-know- the-answer-to looks, "how do you know what Holy Spirit is saying any other time? How did you know the names during your fast? How did you know that God wanted you to come back from America? You know your Father's voice, Rebekah."

I sighed and smiled, and soon I was getting on with the rest of my day. That evening, I was browsing my Facebook page, and I happened upon a post by Hope, the missionary at the International School from all those years ago. I clicked on her name, and was surprised to find myself not looking at her posts, but at her friends. There was a name at the very top of that list— a girl named Tatiana.

Tatiana was Hope's niece, but I only knew that from Facebook. Though I had never met her before, I could feel that prompting of Holy Spirit to send her a message.

So I did.

"Hi Tatiana! I am one of Hope's friends. How can I pray for you?"

"Hi Rebekah! I would really appreciate it if you would pray for me as my husband is trying to get a good job in India! Thank you for reaching out to me!"

The conversation continued over the next four months, with her sending prayer requests and me praying for her and sending back Bible verses. They started off as encouragement, but they very quickly became verses that Holy Spirit would whisper to me, things like feeding the poor or loving your neighbor. I would send them to Tatiana, and she would do whatever the verse said. As the time drew near for her husband's job, I was reassured over and over again by the Holy Spirit that he had nothing to worry about, and sure enough, he landed the interview and got the job.

One morning, a while later, Tatiana and I were recounting the story together. It was good hearing again how God had moved in her life, and it was fun knowing that God had used me to be a part of it. When we got to the end, she looked at me for a moment and asked, "And do you know who the prophet was that made all this happen?"

"No," I answered, surprised that she hadn't mentioned this prophet before.

"You, Rebekah!"

I sat stunned for a moment before I made all the connections in my head. Yes, I had played the role of a prophet in all this— and all of this happened right after I asked Jesus for the gift of prophecy! How good our God is!

Our relationship lasted for years after that, and I helped pray her through renting an apartment and two baby boys, both of whom doctors said would be impossible for her to conceive. With each new word that I got for her, and each victory she experienced in her life, I continued to grow in my confidence that God really did speak to me.

## What Do You Desire?

"I just want to go back to Minnesota, Pastor Seif," I told him over the phone, "I just want to be able to talk about Jesus and not be followed, to read my Bible and not worry about someone finding it, to become more like Jesus and not end up with a gun pointed at my head."

"And I assume you've been praying about this?" Pastor Seif asked.

"Yes! I've been praying about this for so long and nothing has happened!"

"Well," he answered with his level voice, "maybe it's time to start fasting. If you want it that badly, and you think God's in it, but praying isn't making it happen, there might just be a lot of warfare against it. And if God's not in it, then he can make it clear while you fast."

And thus began my second fast. This one lasted forty days, though it wasn't a daily fast. I fasted twice a week, from midnight to five o'clock, just like last time. I would eat no food, nor drink any liquids until the fast was over.

Spiritually, that was an amazing time for me. I felt like Jesus was so close, I could feel him breathing. I began to understand so much more of his heart for me and for the people around me, and I was so aware of his love and it encouraged me so much.

Physically, however, I wasn't doing as well. We had agreed on the partial fast, twice a week, because I have never been the epitome of health, and this was my first long fast. The first day was always harder, and I would feel dizzy and fuzzy all day until I ate. At midnight, I would send a text to Pastor Seif, telling him I had begun my fast. When I woke up, I would anoint myself with oils. I would go through the rest of my day, simply telling my family I wasn't hungry, and carrying around the water bottle I always carried, but watering plants instead.

Day one. Day eight. Day fourteen. Day nineteen. Day twenty-six. Day thirty-three. Day thirty-seven.

Day forty.

I knew something had changed on day forty, that something holding me back from Minnesota had broken. I just didn't know what. Inside me, however, the change was obvious. Beyond becoming more like Jesus, I had surrendered my desire to go back to Minnesota. I still wanted to go, but if Jesus wanted me to wait, then waiting is what I would do.

## The Last Straw

It was now spring of 2014, a whole year since my fast. But that year had not gone by without incident. Since 2000, Mullahs had frequented our doorstep with demands for my imprisonment. Some had even come for my death. But this spring, the intensity heightened. Government agents joined the Mullahs, pressuring my family to hand me over. As it became clear that my whole family was being watched, my father decided that it was time to move.

Our plan worked, for the most part. Changing locations had deterred the Mullahs from lingering on our doorstep. We finally had a moment's respite. But as soon as the Mullahs stopped, another threat soon arose, and that threat was my brother.

The brother who had once declared his love for me, assuring me that nothing would come between us, was gone. Sarmad had fallen in love with his high school sweetheart, a devout Muslim, and his faith was evolving. There were only small shifts at first, but when he left for college in New York, it was as if he had jumped on a water slide.

When we would talk on the phone, he was always agitated, but would never say why. But as months passed, agitation turned to anger, and general anger turned to rage directed at me. He could hardly stop himself from bringing up the evils of Christianity or how I had betrayed my family. Hypocrisy, heresy, and hostility were usually at the top of the list, but any number of things could come up. It never took long for the Quran to come up, or for my status as an infidel. He was angry at me for throwing so many wrenches in his life, and in some ways he was right. I was not one of many marks against him; I was all the marks against him.

Now it was 2014, and Sarmad had finally come back home. But this was no longer the Sarmad who had once comforted me. This was the Sarmad who loved Allah and his wife with a fierce passion, and I was now in the way more than ever. They had moved back into my father's house, where I was still living, and soon, a new baby girl joined us.

There were now six of us in the same house. Sarmad and his family stayed upstairs, my parents on the main floor, and I in the basement. Eshe, Sarmad's daughter, was the most precious baby girl in the whole world. No tension between my brother and I could take away the love I had for this sweet child. I would often go upstairs to sit with Eshe and sing to her all my favorite songs, like "Twinkle Twinkle Little Star."

One afternoon, I was climbing the stairs to go sing with my niece again. I had had "Onward Christian Soldiers" stuck in my head all morning, and I couldn't help but sing my own version as I trod upwards.

"Onward Christian Soldiers, marching up the stairs. . ." I was feeling pretty proud of my clever rendition, when I rounded the last corner and a looming figure blocked the stairs. "Hey Sarmad," I began, my stomach already clenched, "I was just going to go sing to Eshe." I held up an empty cookie tin I was planning on using as a drum, as if I needed evidence of my plan.

"No."

"Alright," I said as I turned back around and started heading down the stairs again, hoping to avoid another shouting match with Sarmad. I hardly noticed that I had started humming my song again until Sarmad spoke.

"Rebekah," he said, his voice strained like caged thunder, "Stop singing that song."

I nodded but kept walking. I knew the situation was serious— Sarmad was livid— but it felt a little bit like when we were kids, annoying each other and trying to see how far we could go before he told mom.

I rounded the corner and continued down the stairs, waiting until I was out of earshot before continuing my song.

"Onward Christian Soldiers, marching down the stairs. . ." the muted words slipped through the slight grin on my face. I was almost to the next corner of the staircase when I heard pounding footsteps behind me.

*"I told you to stop singing that song!"* There was no restraint in Sarmad's voice now. I started running down the stairs, all thoughts of childish prodding gone. I was in danger.

I felt his hand grab my arm and then it was being yanked behind me, throwing off my balance. My feet stumbled for a moment, barely catching myself on the stairs before I was being pushed downwards again. Sarmad kept up his pace, not slowing while I tumbled down the stone stairs, each bone in my ankle aching and throbbing when it slammed into a stair. We burst through my bedroom door and with a final shove I landed facedown on my bed. Sarmad was in a frenzy now, his fists pounding into my body. We were both screaming now; me begging him to stop and him roaring curses at me. My whole body was throbbing, and just as my spine felt as though it was about to snap, there was a hesitation. I opened my eyes and gasped softly, for Mama was here. Now it would stop. She walked through the doorway and into the room, stopping right behind my brother. Sarmad had paused to see what she would do, but she remained still.

"Please, Sarmad," I said softly, "stop."

But he didn't.

## The Dams Break

I have no idea how long the beating lasted, but I do know that neither said a word when they left, and neither acknowledged it in the following days. But while they wouldn't say anything about it, my body bore witness. The spinocerebellar ataxia I had been diagnosed with back in 1998 had been mostly latent, but after this latest beating, my health began declining rapidly. My hands began shaking, my legs became weak, and my speech became slurred. Simple tasks became nearly impossible without help, and each doctor's appointment confirmed that there was nothing we could do.

Not long after all of this, my father approached me with a question.

"Rebekah, what do you want?"

"I want to go back to my Minnesota!" I exclaimed.

He paused for a moment to think. "Well, if you can find somewhere to stay in three days, then I will help you get there."

I couldn't believe it. This was the first time I had real hope about going back to Minnesota in years! I rushed to our computer and sent out messages to everyone I knew, explaining the deal and asking for anyone to house me. I waited all night, and all the second day without any responses. But I took hope from the Resurrection and remembered that the disciples too didn't hear anything until the third day. And what a fitting story— for on the third day, mere minutes before the deadline was up, I got a response back from friends in Minnesota, offering a place to stay. My father honored our agreement, and on September 11th, 2014, I arrived back in Minnesota.

When I tell people about how I came back to America, my simple answer is Jesus. It took miracles for me to come back, from my passport being marked to never leave the country, to my parents allowing me to return to the country where I found Jesus. He has been gracious far beyond what I deserve, and I am forever thankful as I live in the land I was forbidden to return to.

# CHAPTER EIGHT:
# THE JOURNEY CONTINUES

*He who keeps a fig tree will eat of its fruit, and whoever*
*protects their master shall be honored.*
*Proverbs 27:18*

From the spring of 2014 when my health started declining until January of 2018, I was bound to a walker. Once I was back in Minnesota, I began going to physical therapy and regaining the ground that I had lost in speech and walking.

While I had made a lot of progress, I was still unable to walk at all without a walker. However, on January 27th of 2018, I went to a Revival conference in the Twin Cities. The leaders of the conference prayed for my ears, my spinocerebellar ataxia, and my family, and I am healed in so many ways. Though I still use a walker, it is mostly for balance now, and I was given so much healing in my heart and my soul and my mind. Our God is truly a God of miracles.

Isaiah 53:5 still stands: But He was pierced for our transgressions, He was crushed for our iniquities; upon Him was the chastisement for our peace, and *with His wounds we are healed.* He already paid the price for our sins— but he also paid the price for our hurts. He took on our wounds and our pain so that we could live fully healed, mind, body, and soul, in him. My wounds are being healed because of his wounds.

I am now living in Minnesota, staying with friends, speaking at churches, and loving Jesus. Mama is the only family member I see anymore, as she comes to visit annually. Baba Jee passed away the spring after I left.

I pray that your story goes on the way Jesus has written it, because he is the Alpha and Omega.

I pray that you look towards the cross and embrace suffering, to be sanctified and understand the sufferings of Christ.

I pray that you know the love of our Abba and that you fearlessly make known his name, regardless of the cost.

I pray that you truly believe in how much Jesus has already done for you and how much more he will do, out of his deep love for you.

But most of all, I pray that you love Jesus for the rest of your life.

I pray you love the Comforter, the Healer, the Spirit.

I pray you love the Savior, the Immanuel, our Jesus.

I pray you love the Creator, the Sender, the Father.

The grace of the Lord Jesus be with God's people.

Amen.

# AFTERWORD

By Mary Lene

There are encounters in life that change us. For years I have been in tune with the persecuted Church and Christians who have chosen to lay down their lives to follow Jesus. I've read many testimonies where men, women and children have endured the unthinkable because they count their lives as loss knowing that what is to come far exceeds what they are enduring in this world.

Meeting Rebekah changed me. As I sat and listened to her story unfold, I was in awe of her love for Christ and her obedience and willingness to lay down all that she was for all that He is. As I choked back tears, I found myself seeing some of my favorite scriptures coming alive before my very eyes. Phillipians 3:8-10 "What is more, I consider everything a loss compared to the surpassing greatness of knowing Christ Jesus my Lord, for whose sake I have lost all things. I consider them rubbish, that I may gain Christ and be found in him, not having a righteousness of my own that comes from the law, but that which is through faith in Christ-- the righteousness that comes from God and is by faith. I want to know Christ and the power of his resurrection and the fellowship of sharing in his sufferings, becoming like him in his death, and so, somehow, to attain the resurrection from the dead." As she spoke, this scripture captured her life. Rebekah's story is an example of coming to a place where nothing else will satisfy but Jesus himself. It is a journey that can only be accomplished when we give all that we are for all that he is.

This book is significant. It is a book that expands our understanding of what many have endured and few have had an opportunity to share. It is a book of choices. An example of choosing the road less traveled for a greater reward. It is a book of hope that is shown in the story of our redemption that can only be found in Jesus. When we die to our old nature, it is then we truly live.

Rebekah's heart behind this memoir has always been to present her story as one written by the Lord. She laid down her life long ago trusting that in doing so, the Lord would instruct her tongue and footsteps to glorify Him and give others hope. She offers that same chance and choice to you today. If you do not know Christ as your personal savior, today is the day of salvation. 2 Corinthians 6:2 "For he says, 'In the time of my favor I heard you, and in the day of salvation I helped you.'  I tell you , now is the time of God's favor, now is the day of                                    salvation."

The Lord has a plan for each one of us.  Most of us will not have our story unfold as Rebekah did. But, if we allow our story to be written by the Lord,  he will use it for His Glory, as he is doing with her.   She believed the truth that Jesus died on the cross, shedding his blood for our sins, washing us white as snow so that we can have ever-lasting life with our Heavenly Father and Lord. If you desire to know the Lord,  as your savior, your coming King, do not tarry. Today is the day. Romans 10:13. "Everyone who calls on the name of the Lord will be saved."

Made in the USA
Lexington, KY
09 July 2018